Fantastic
ANIMALS

GRAYSCALE COLORING BOOKS

VOLUME 5.

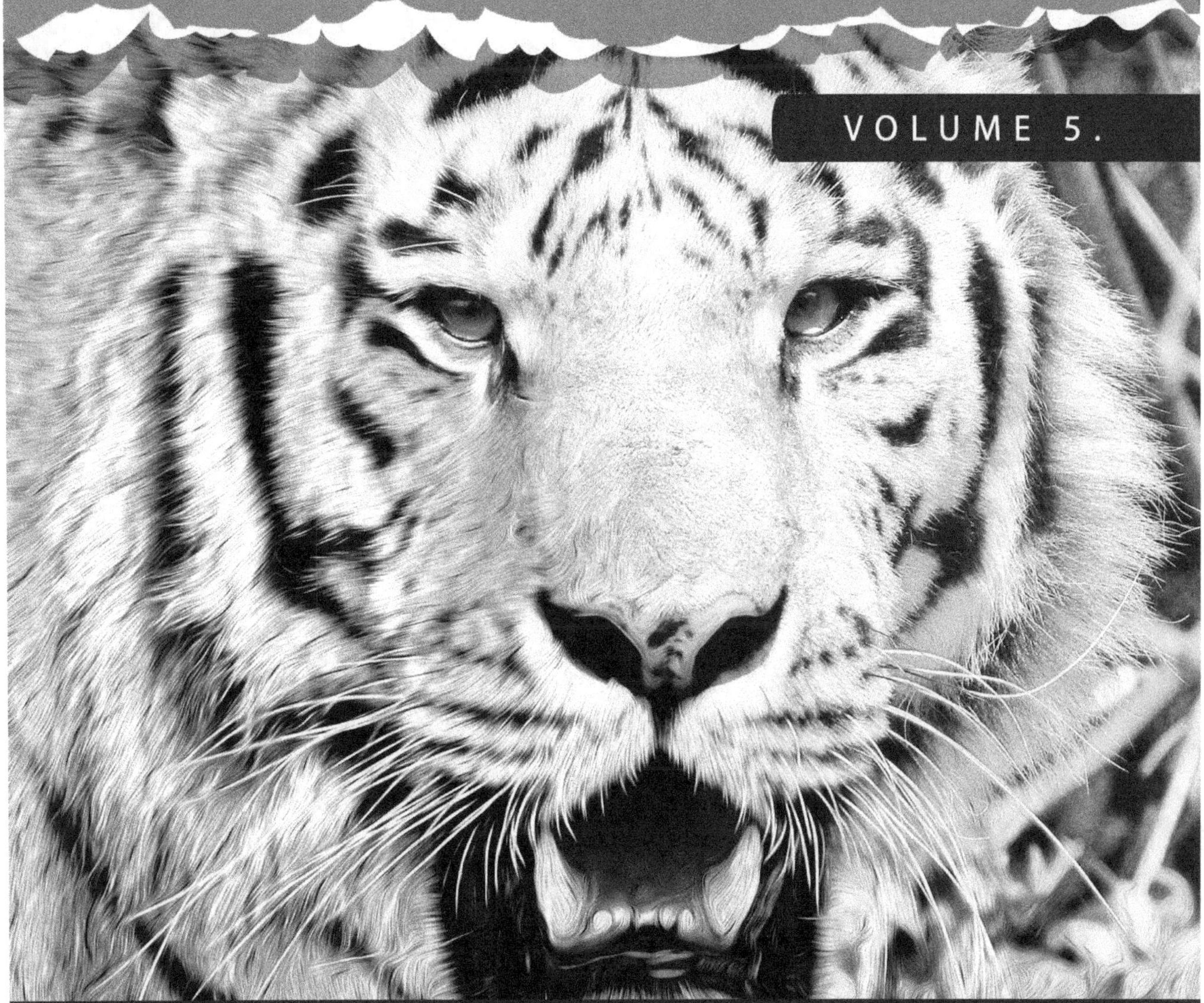

COLOR TEST PAGE

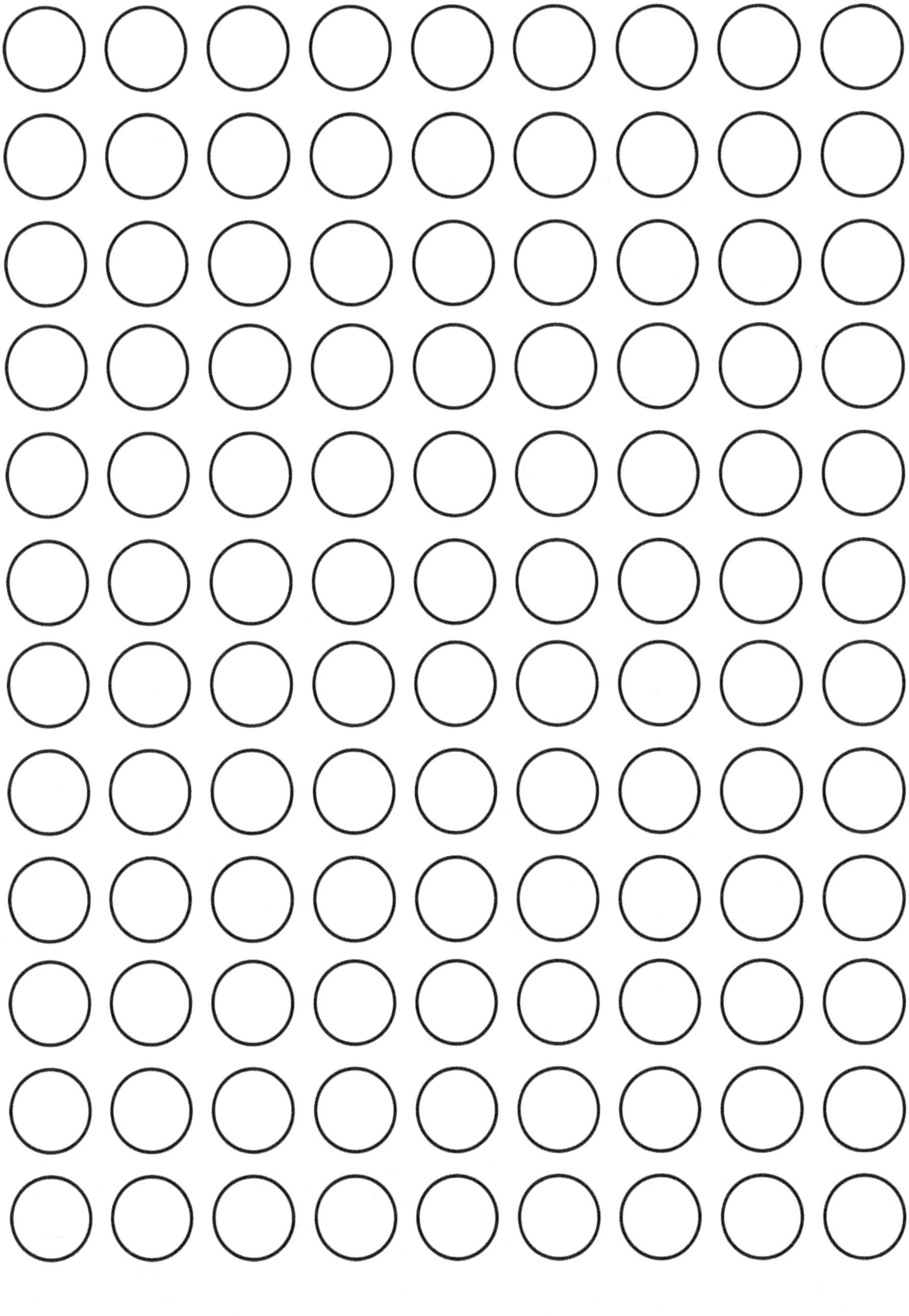

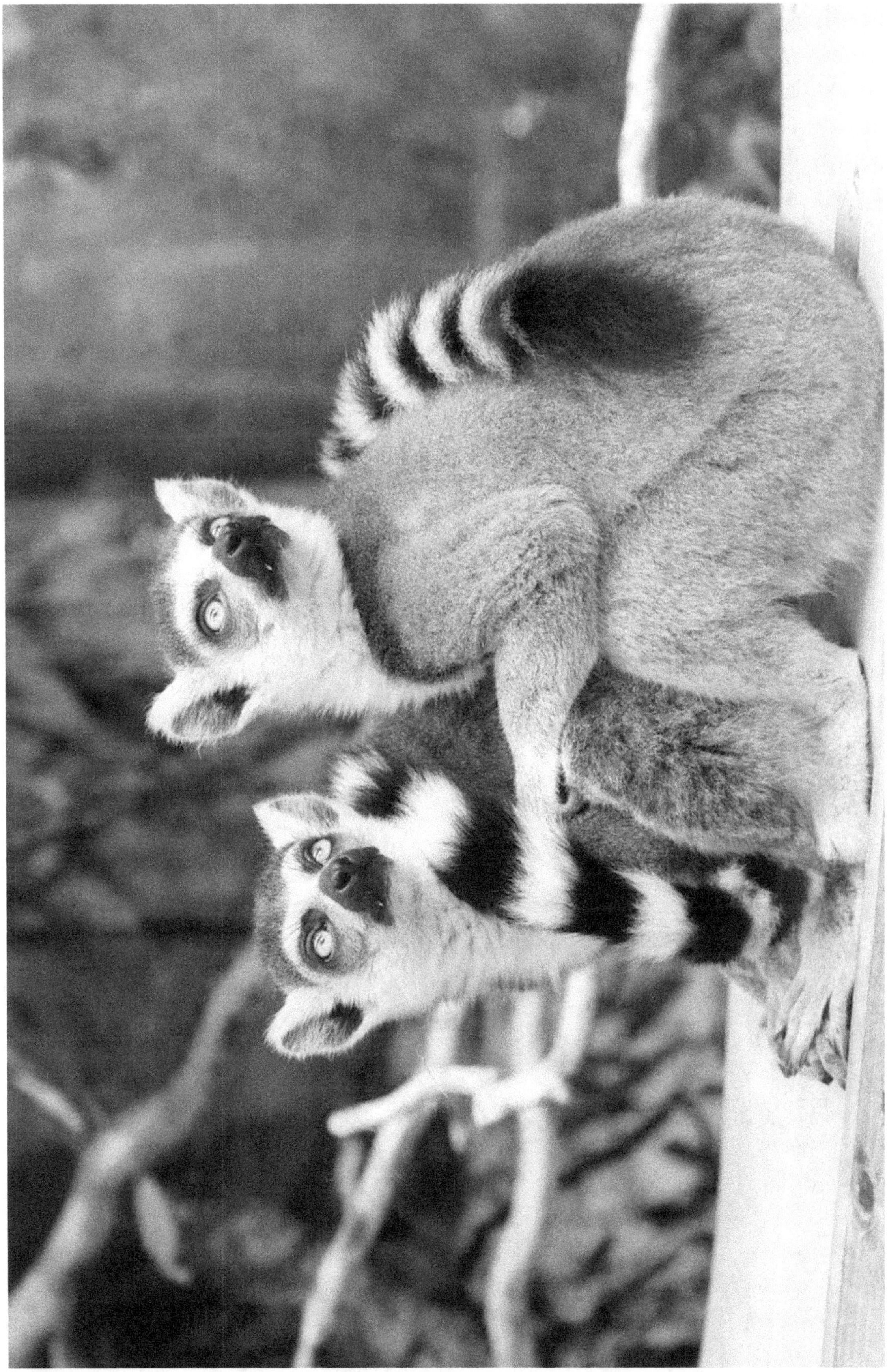

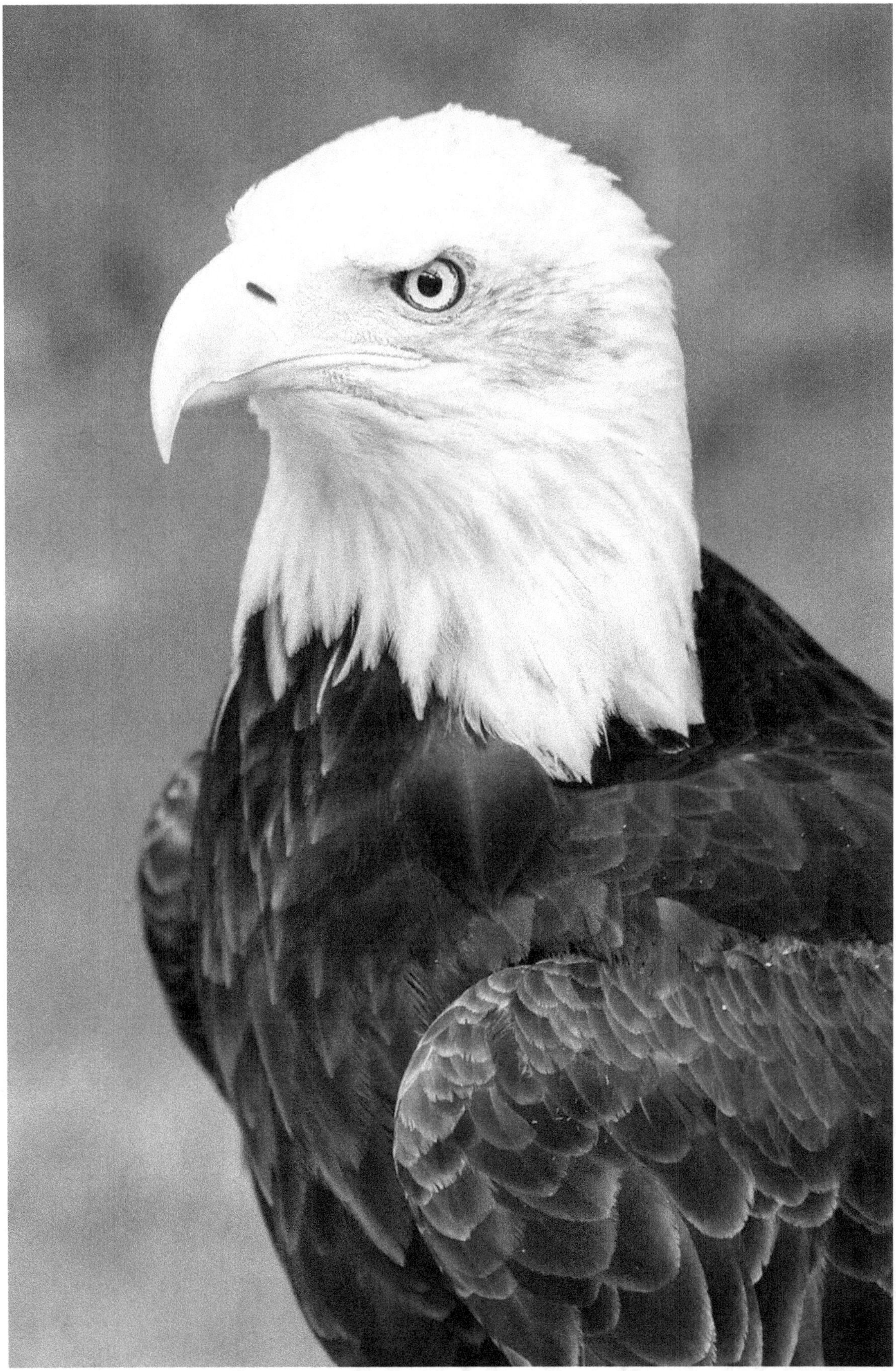

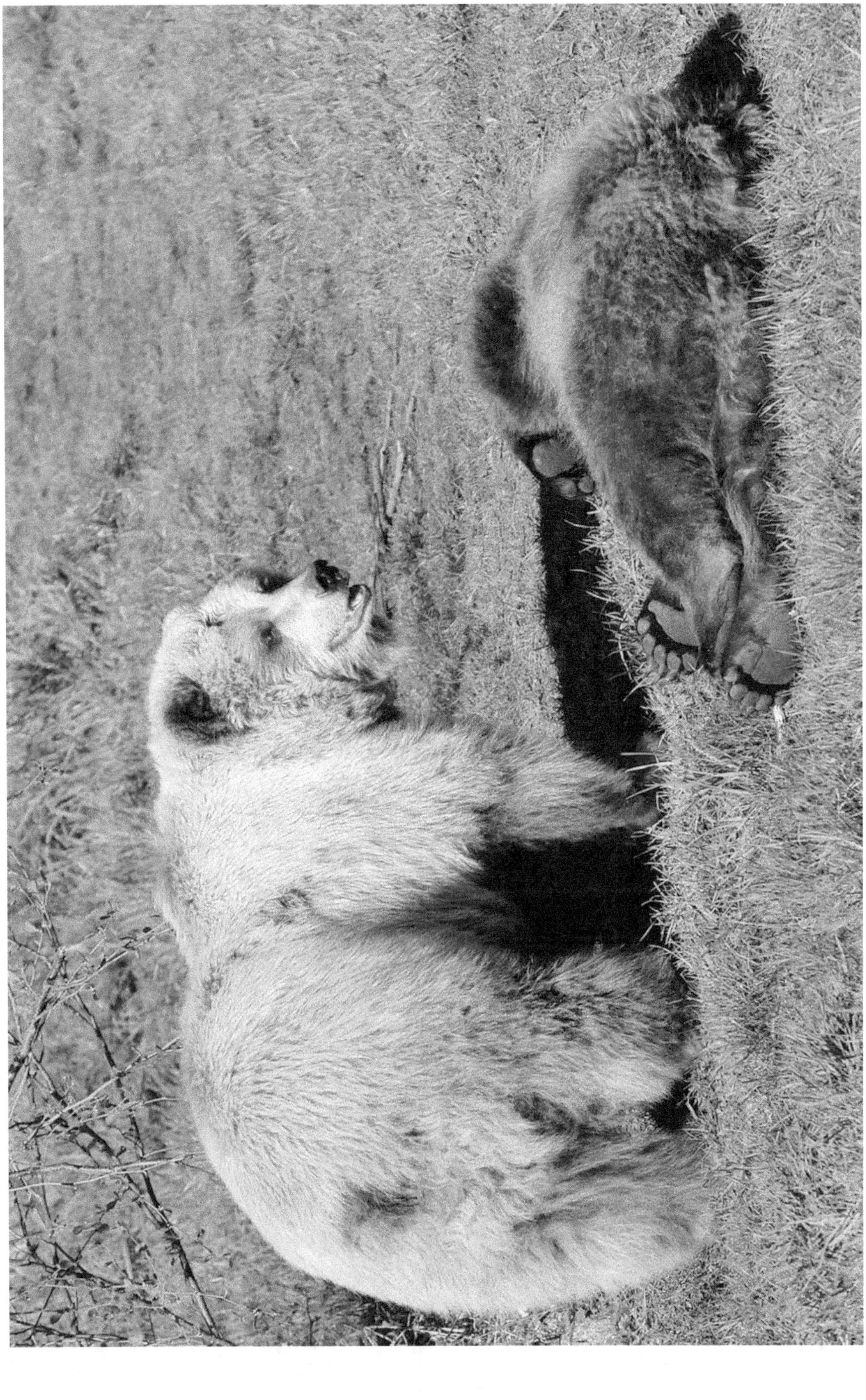

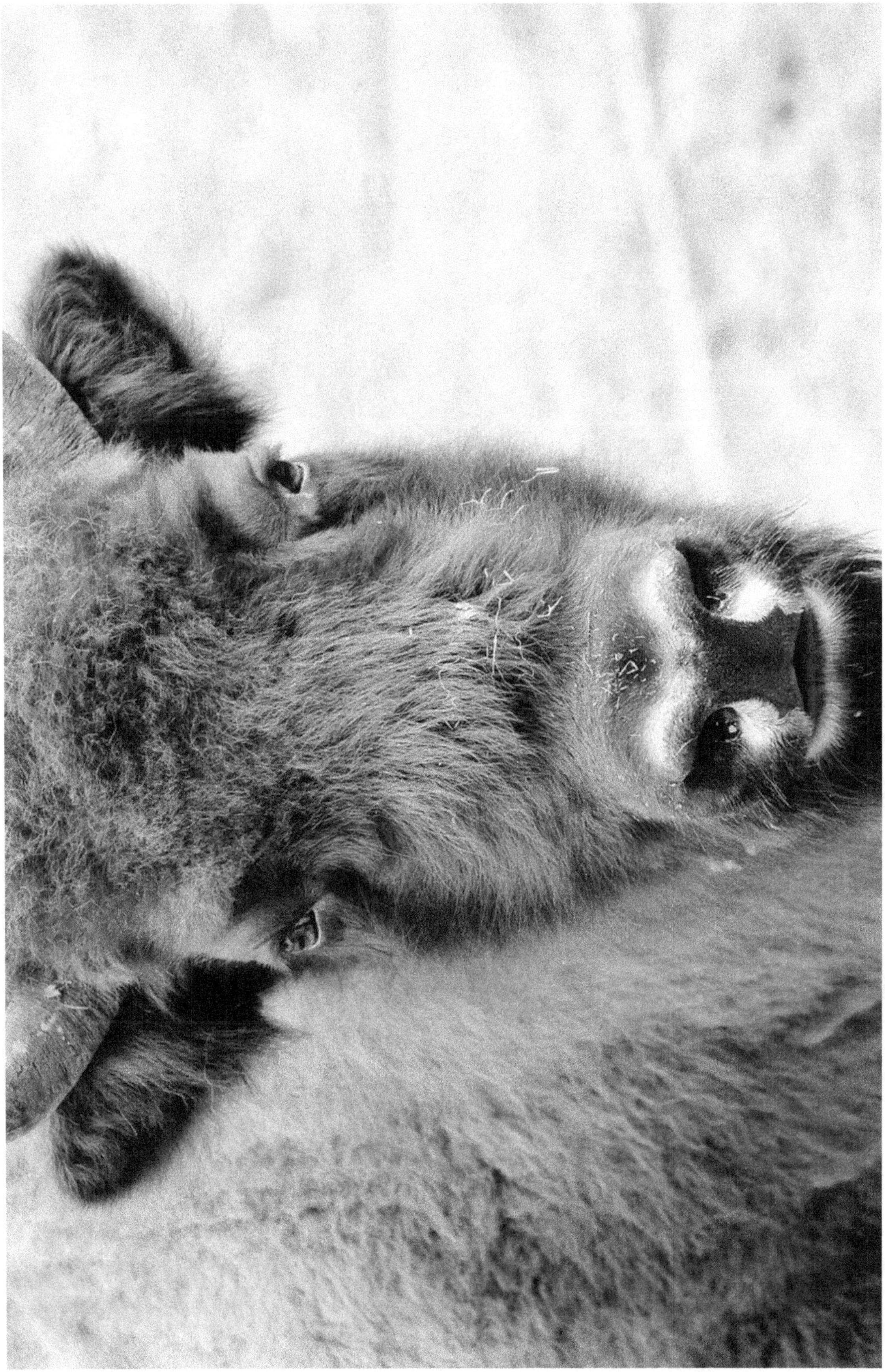

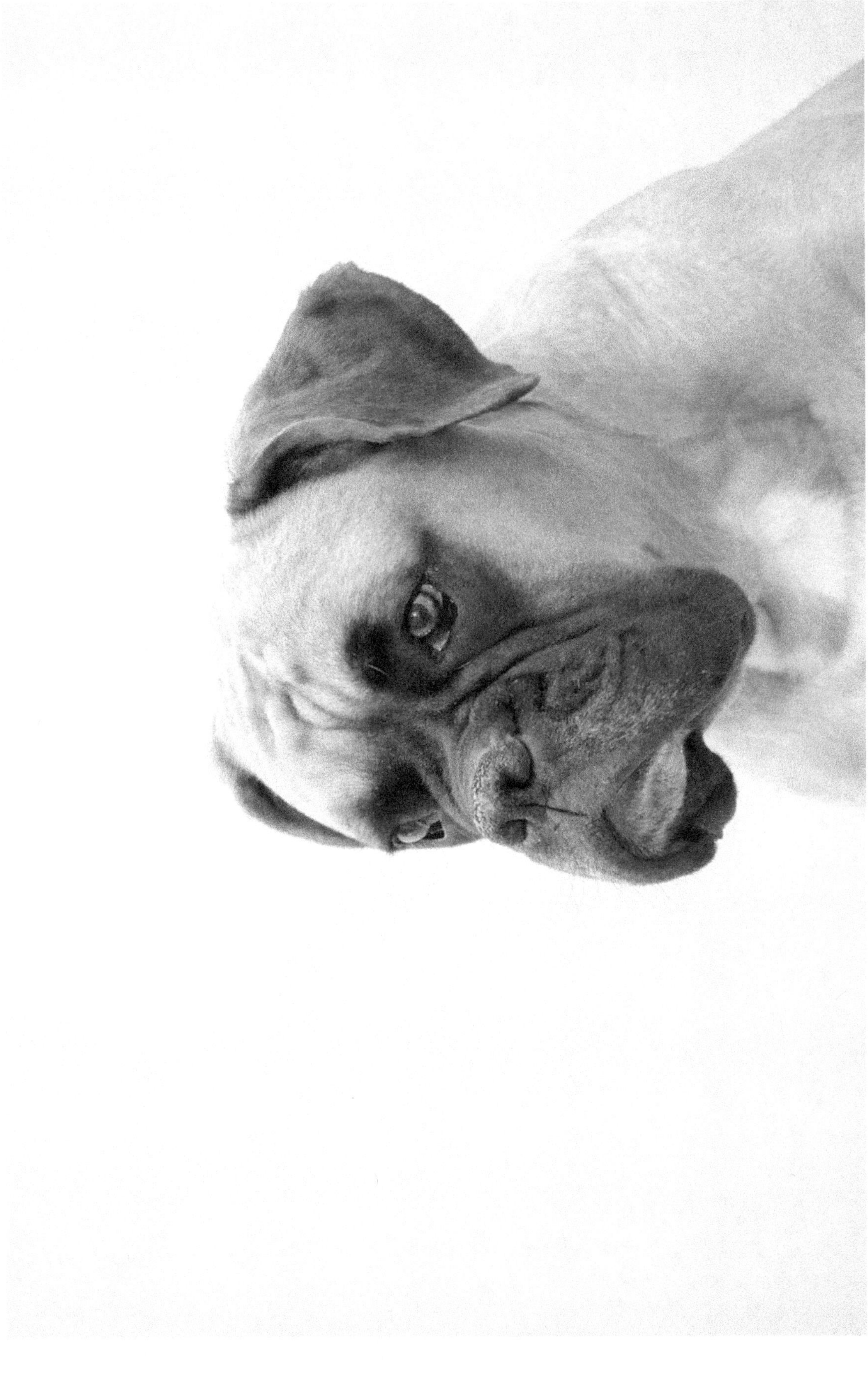

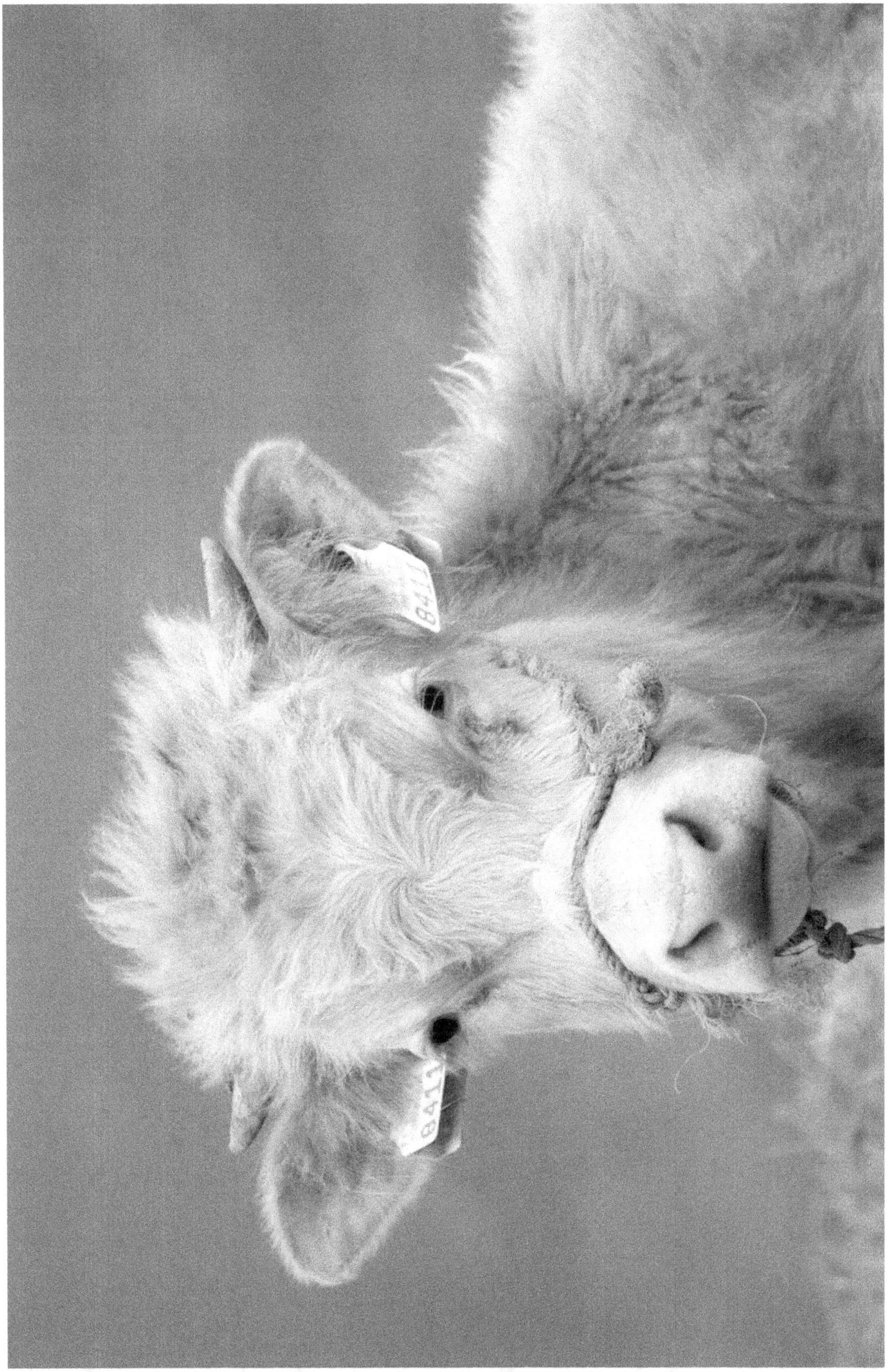
8411

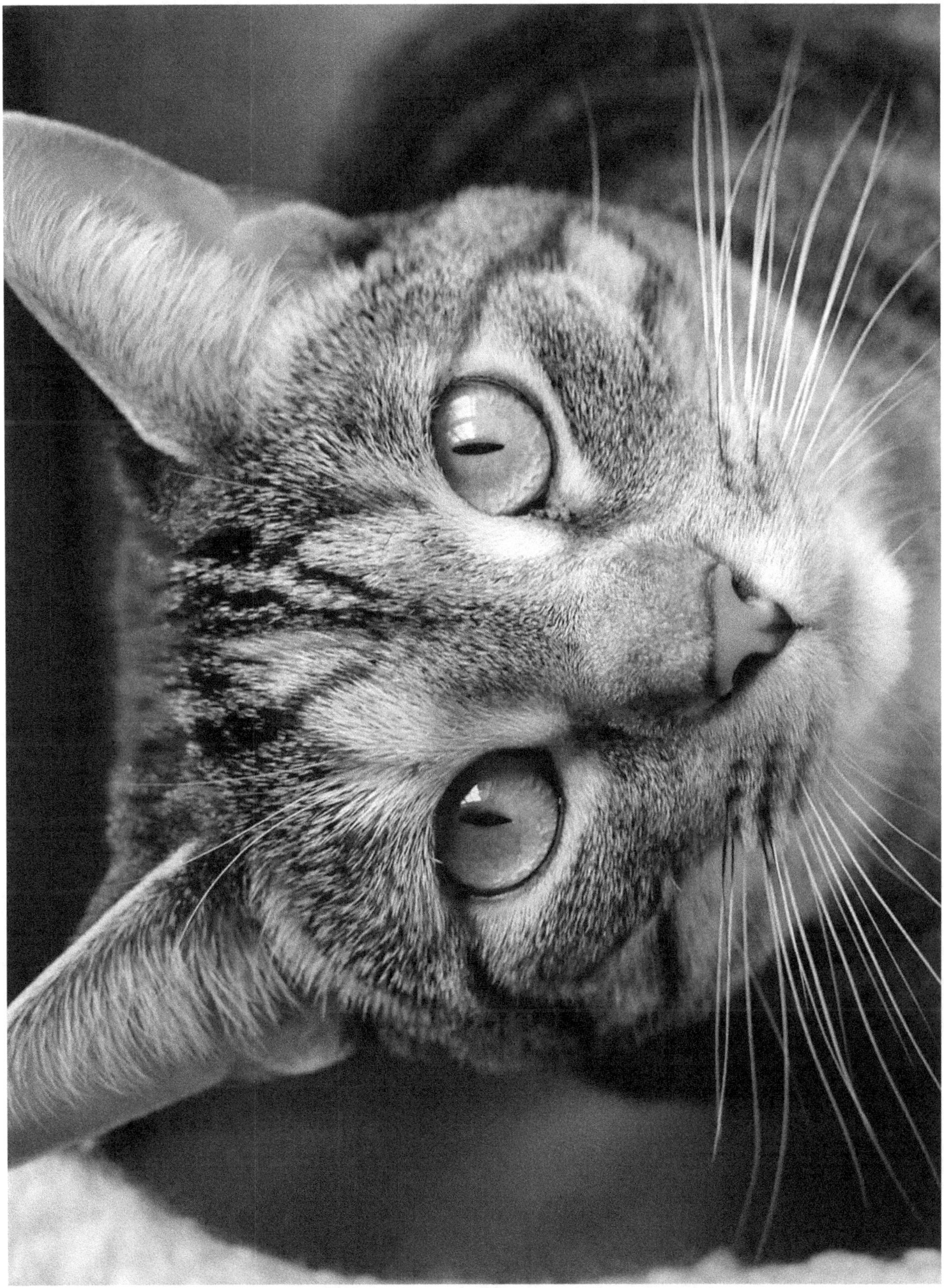

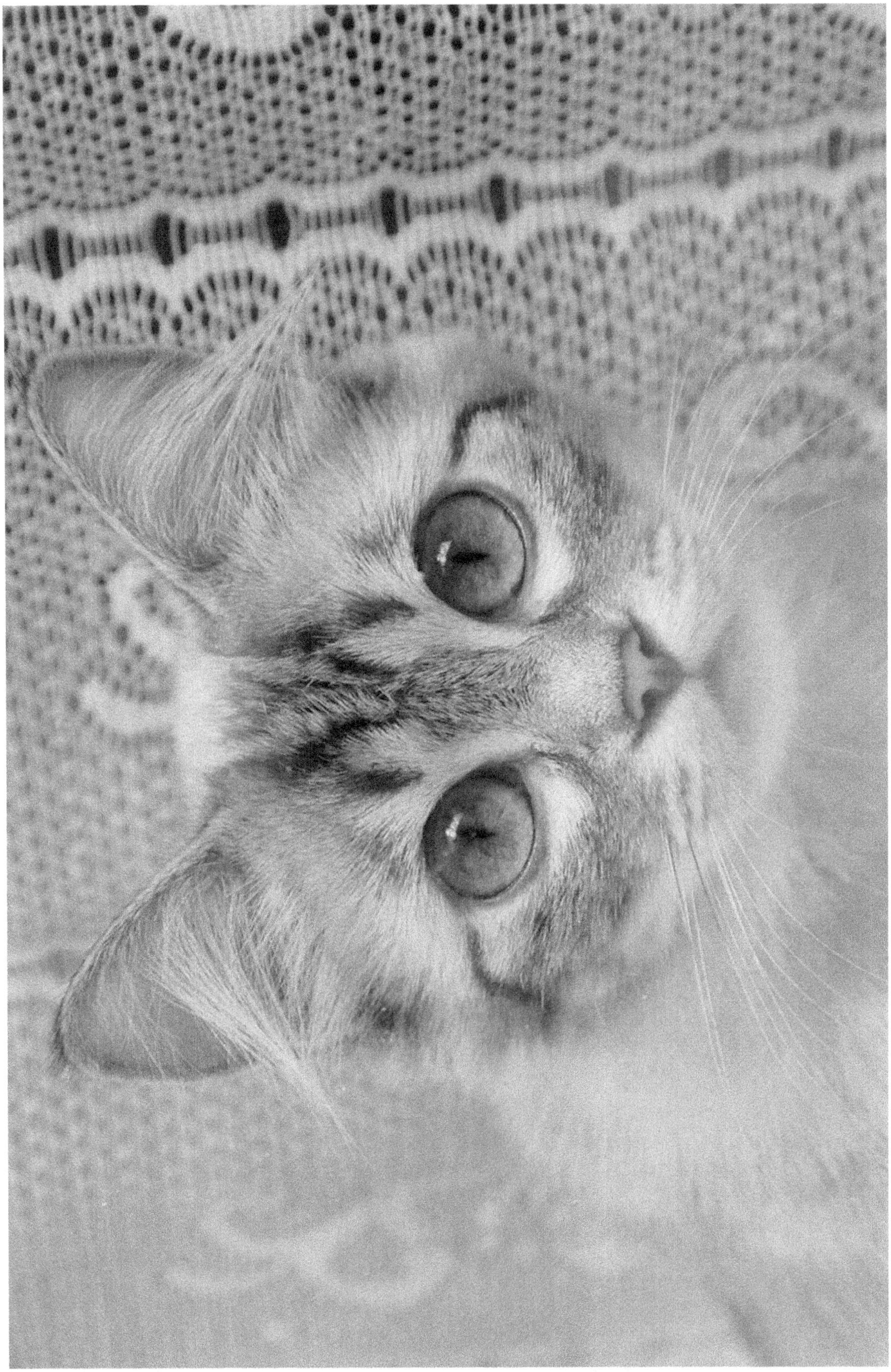

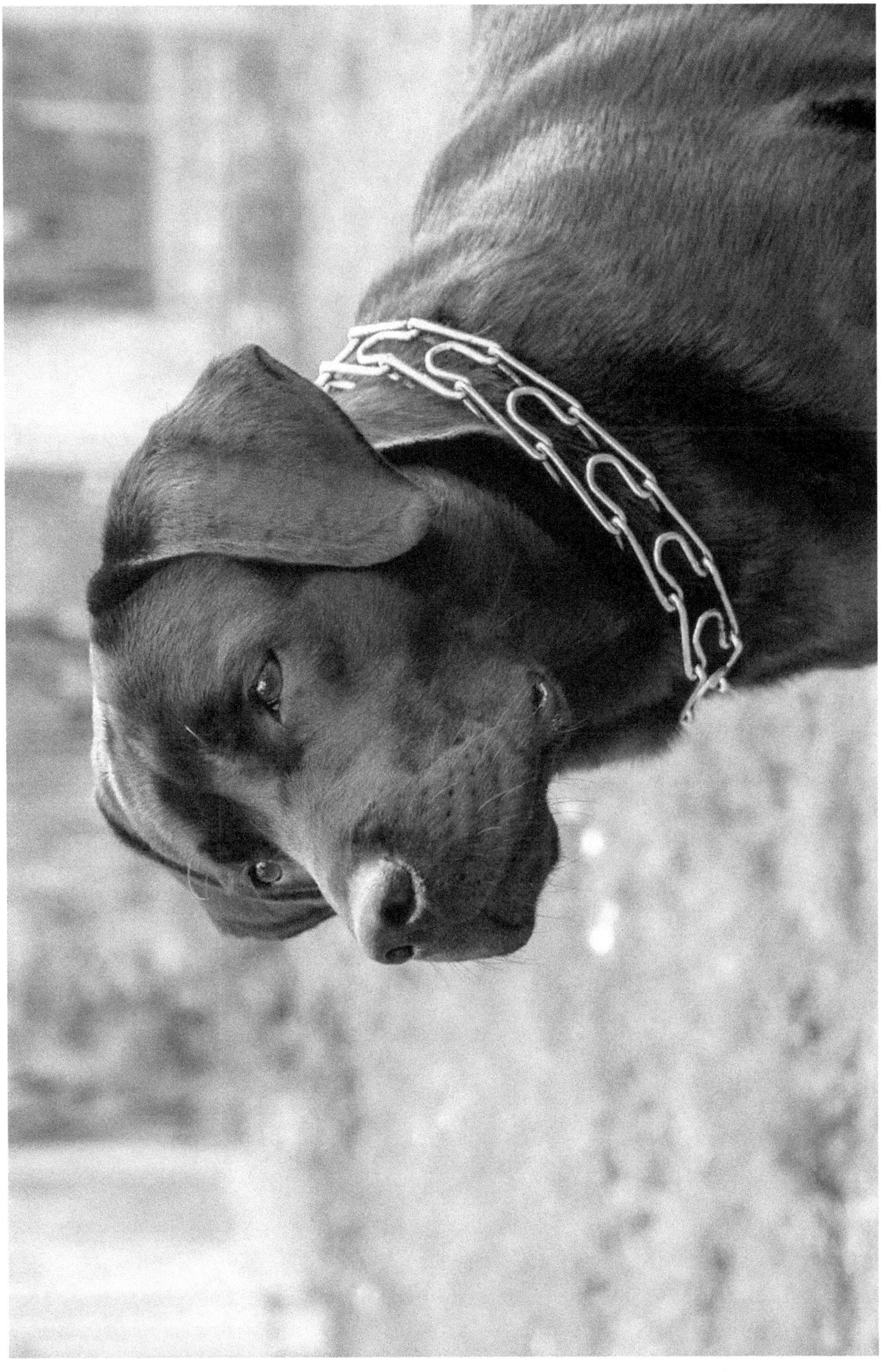

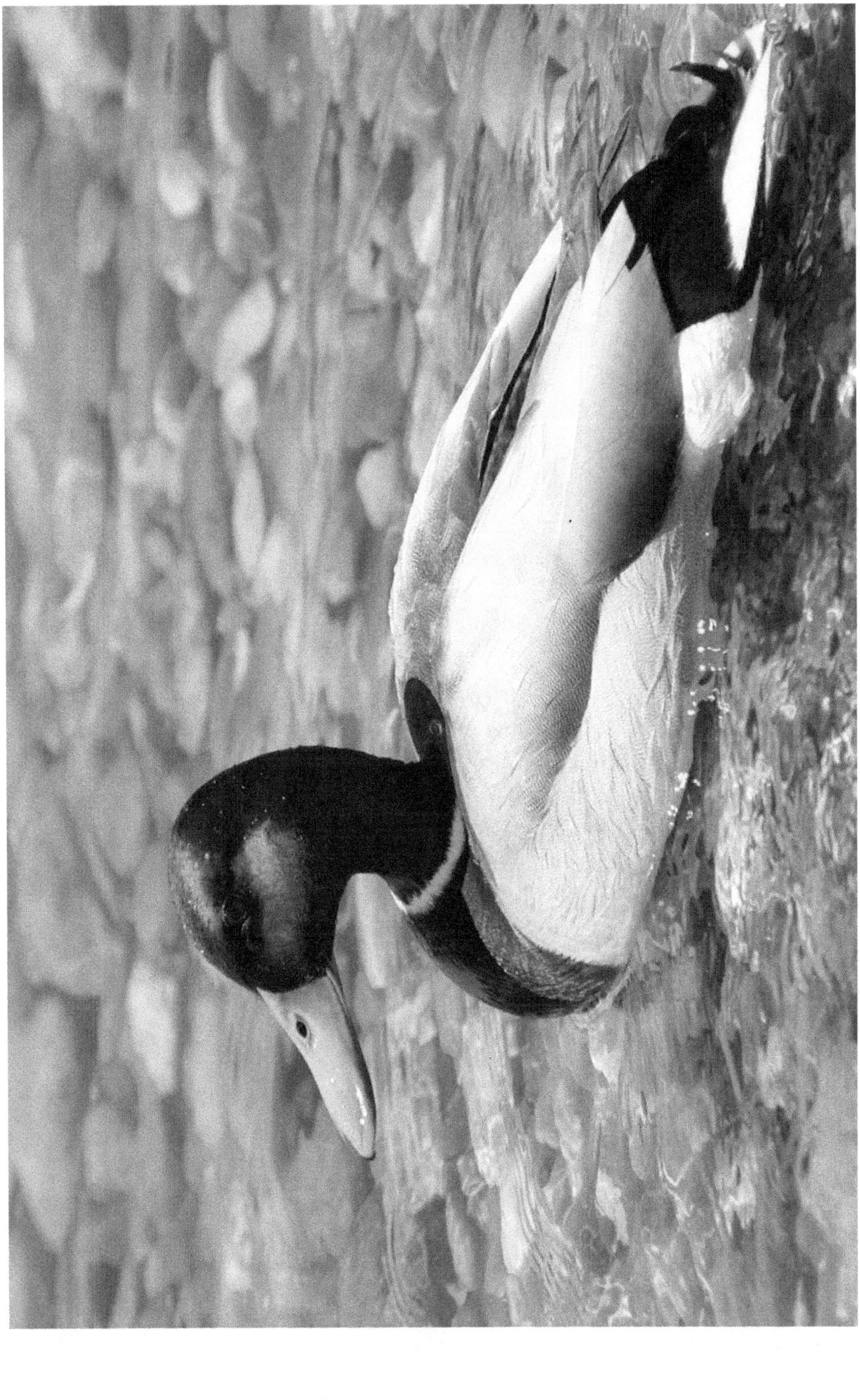

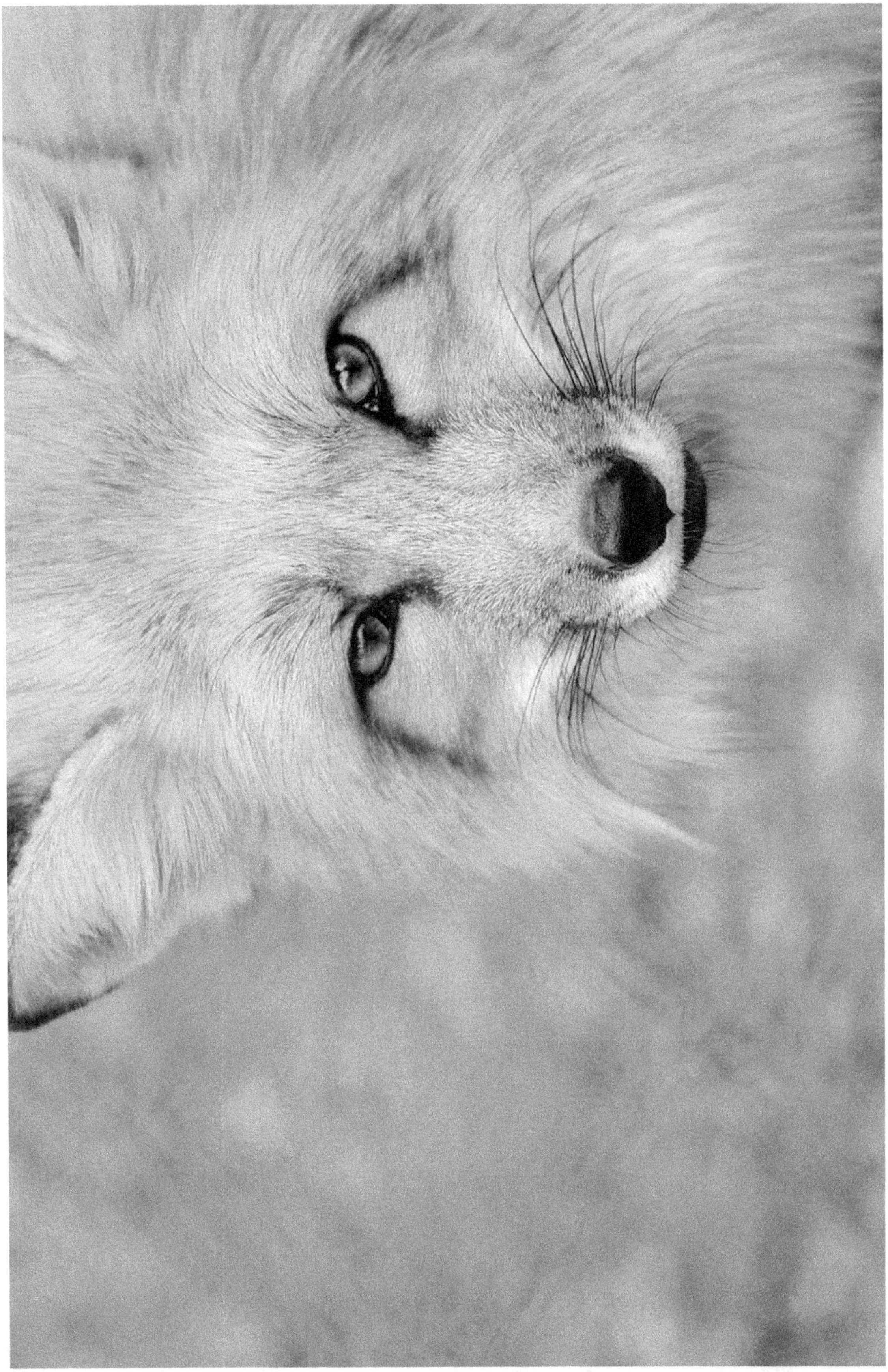

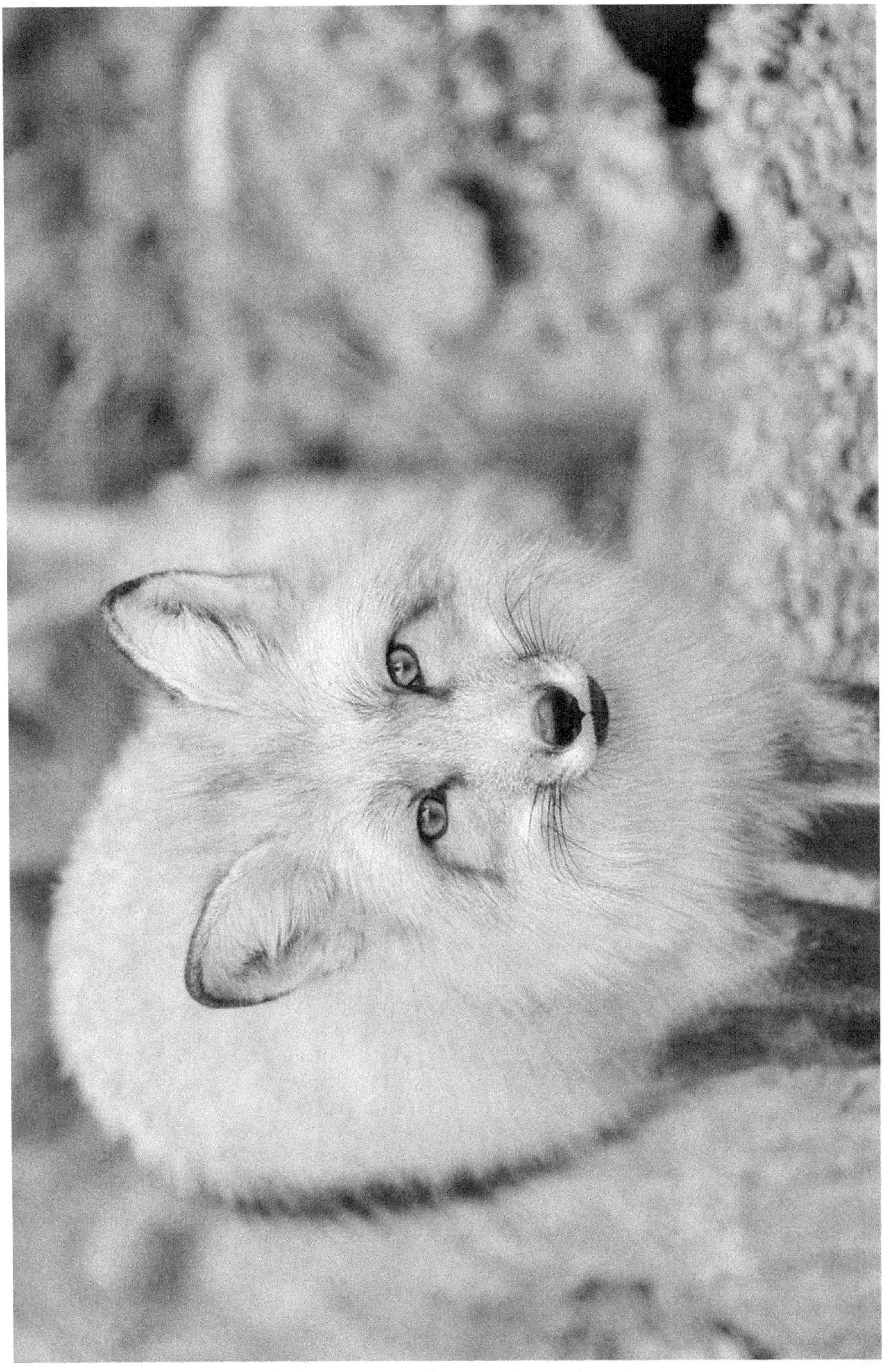

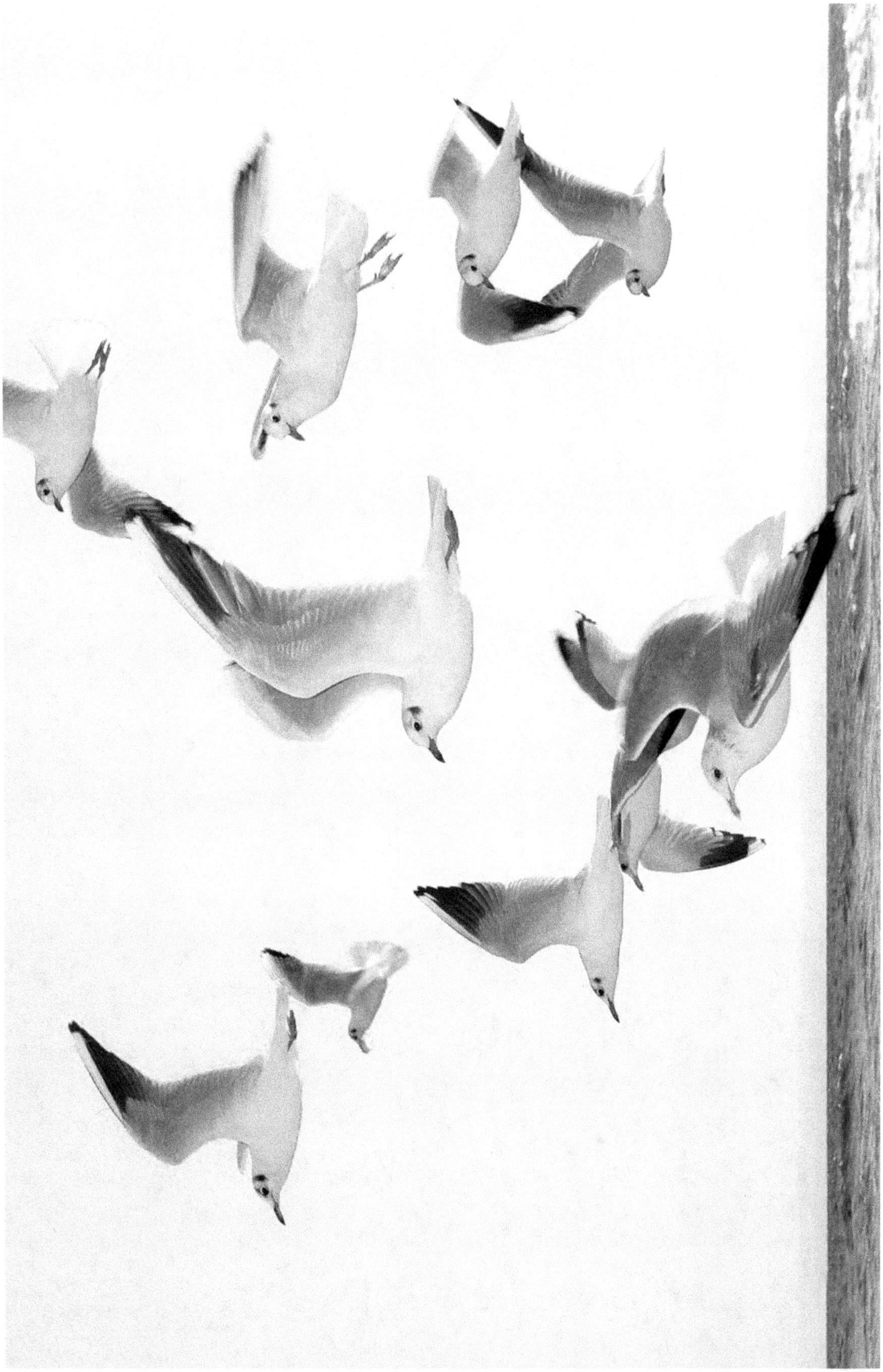

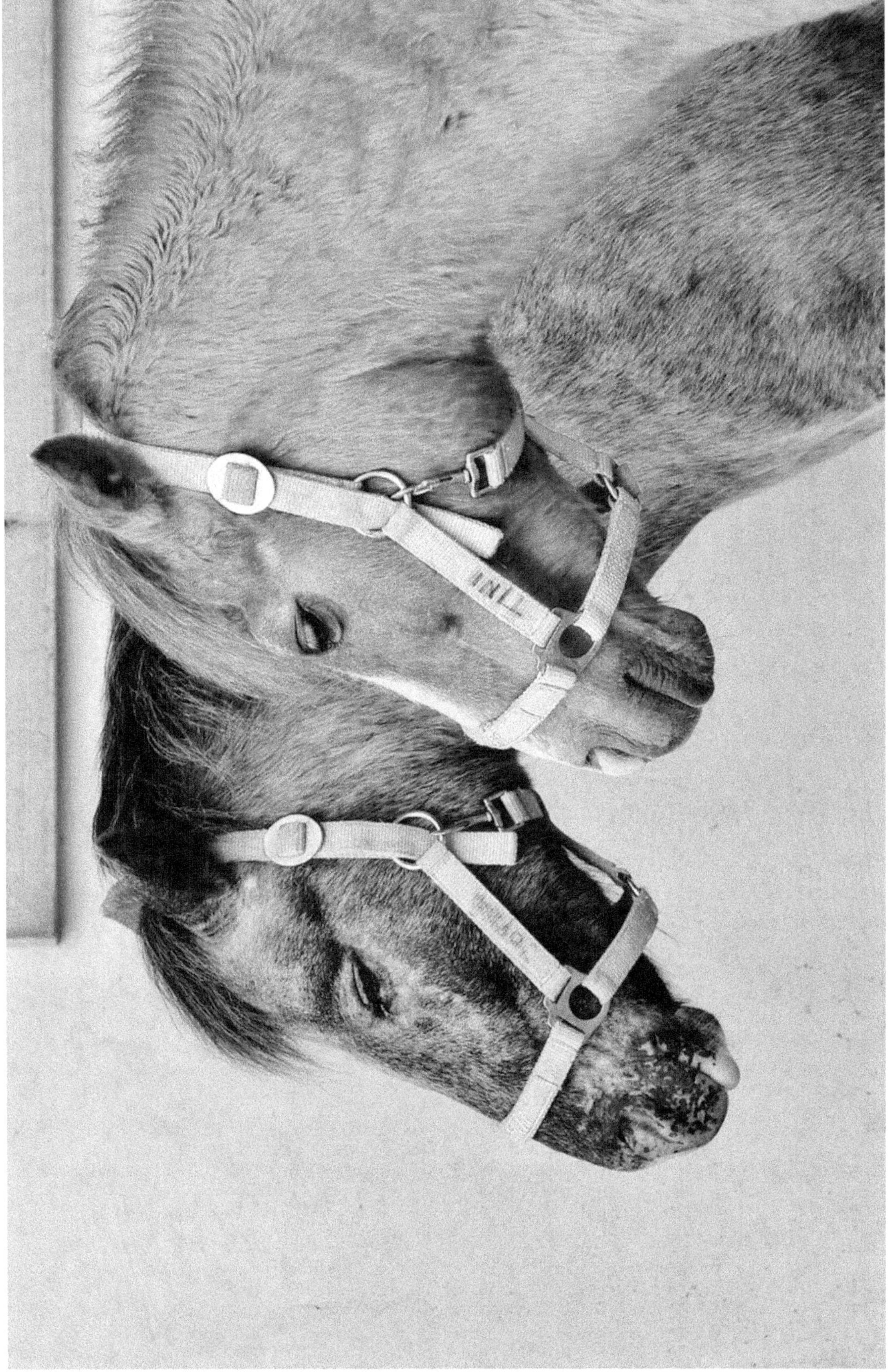

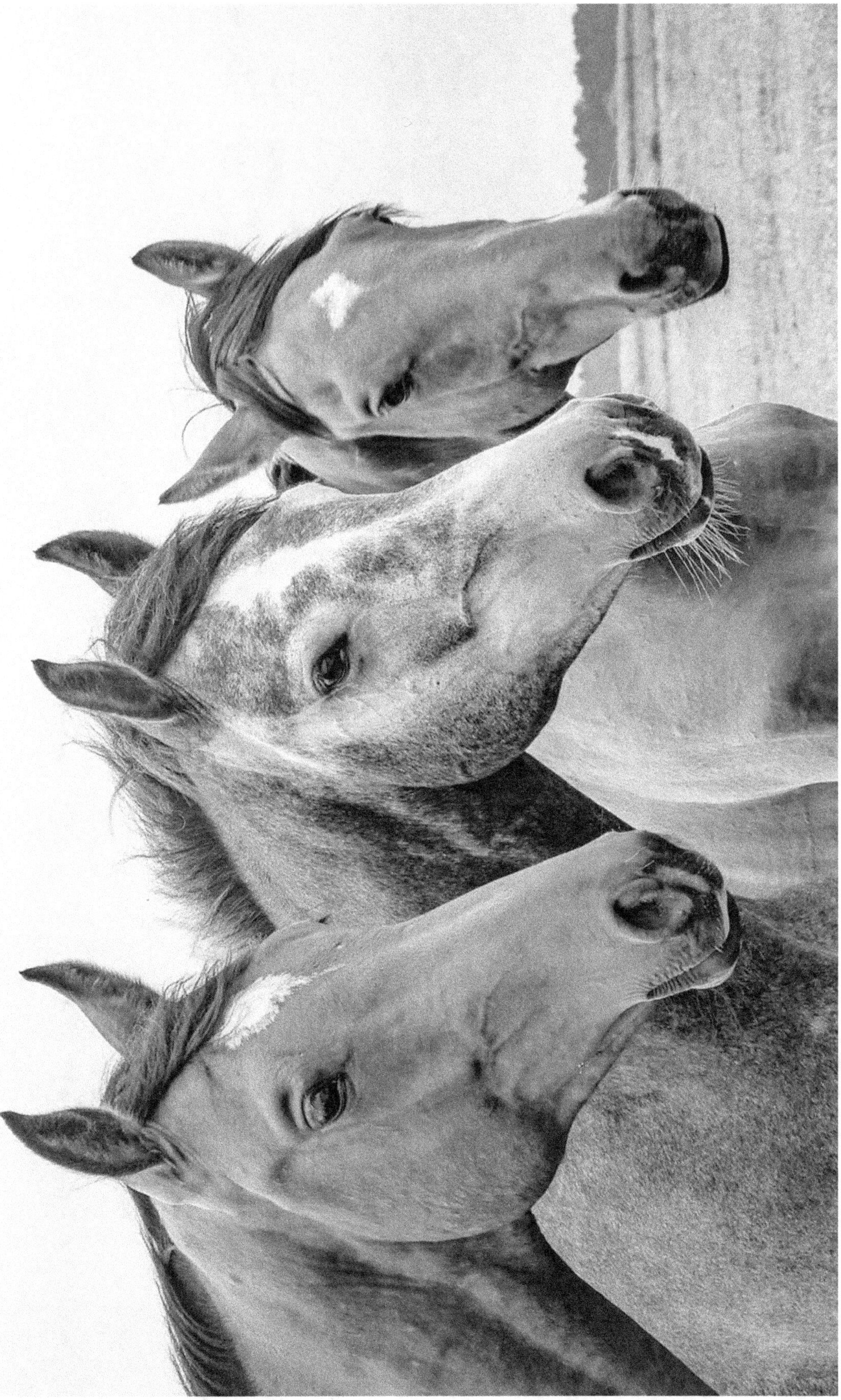

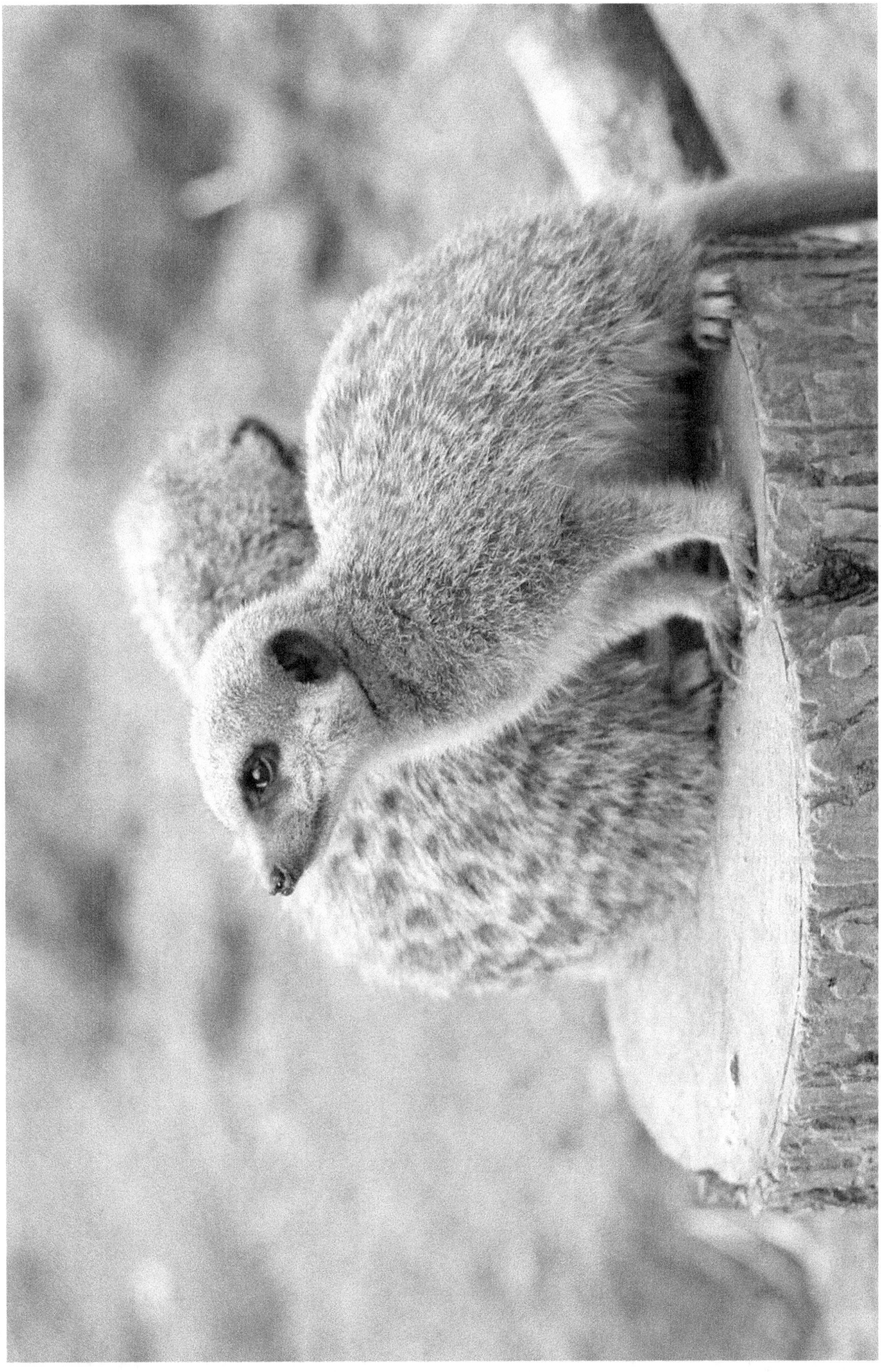

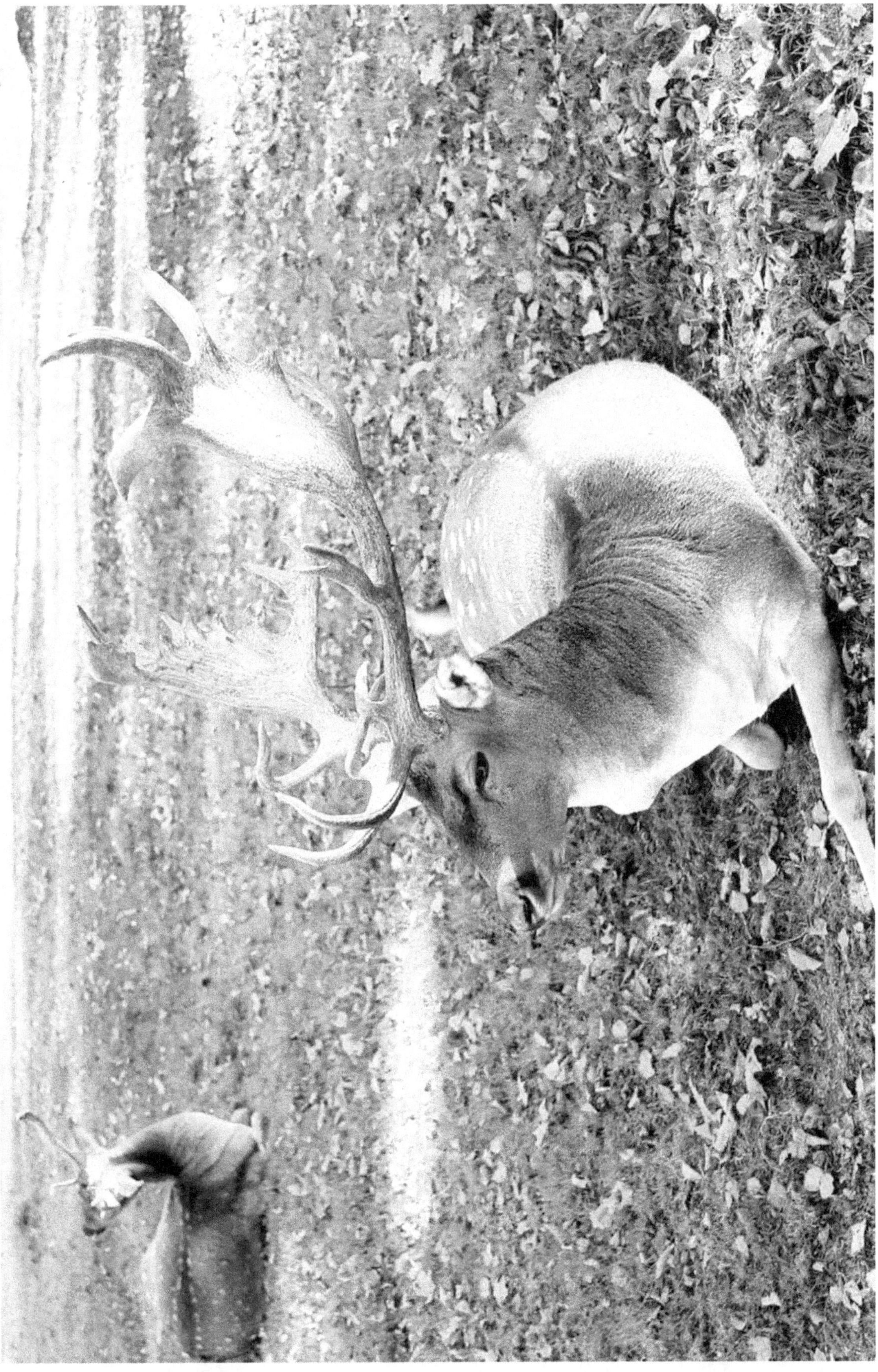

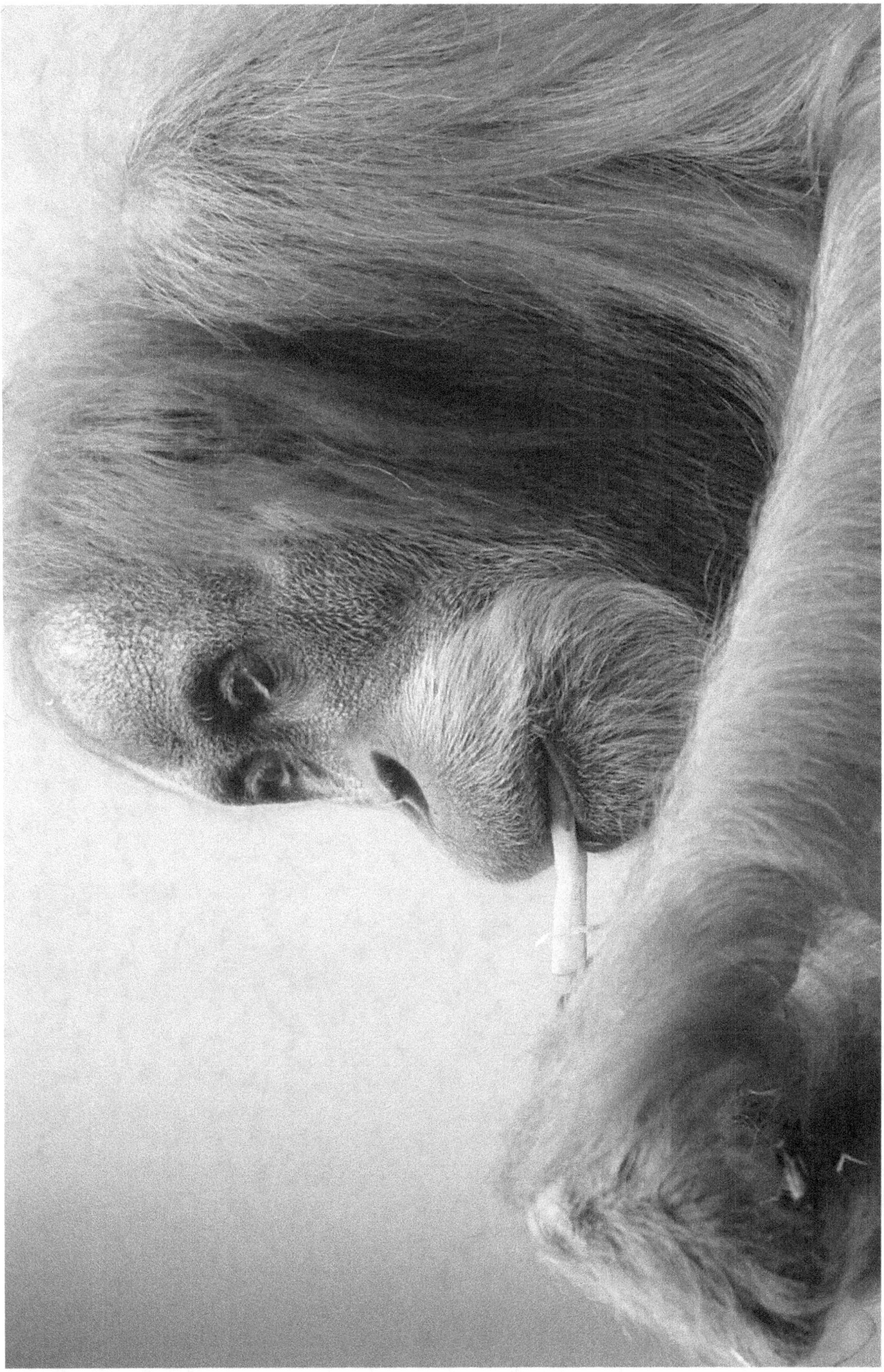

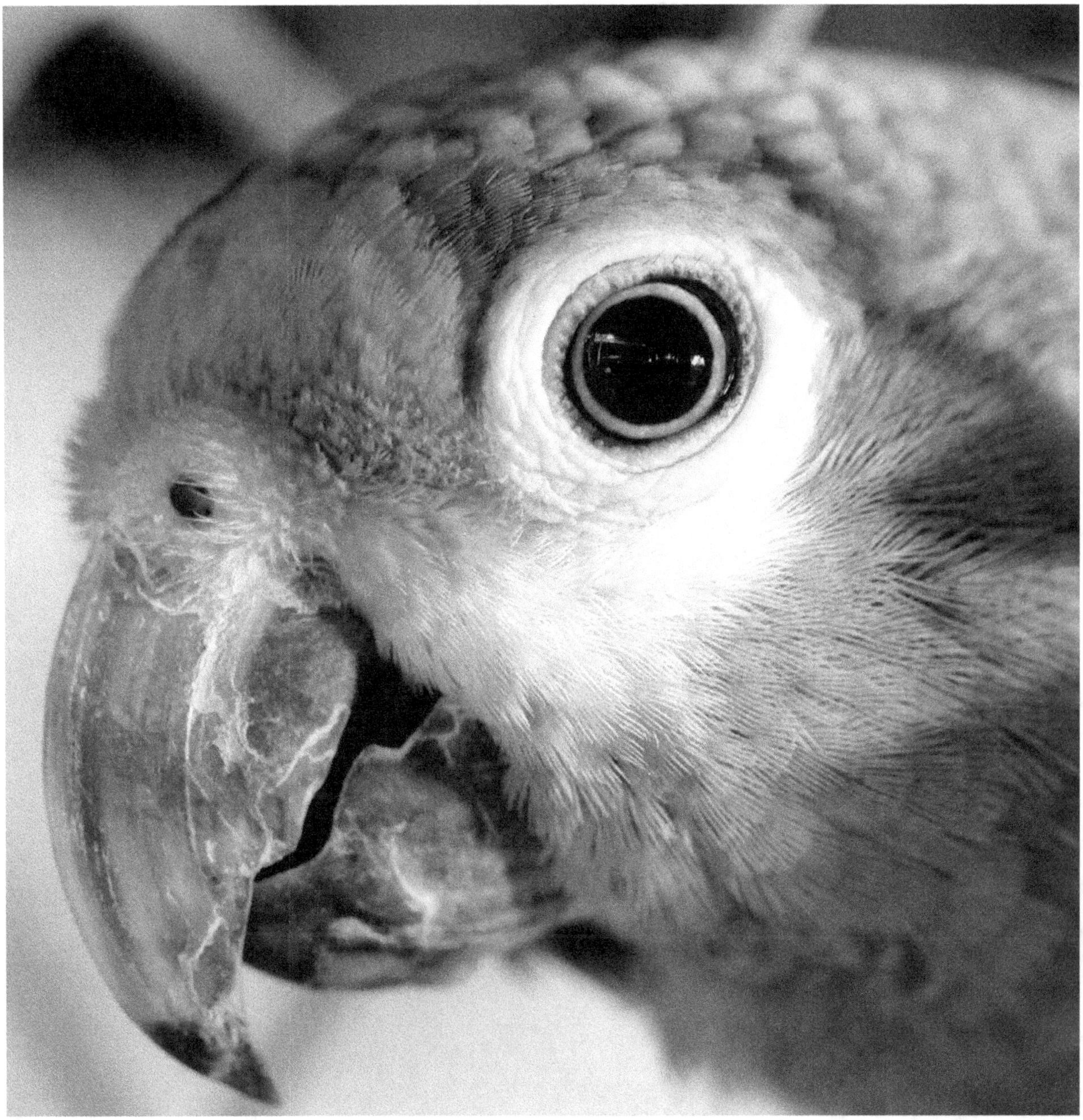

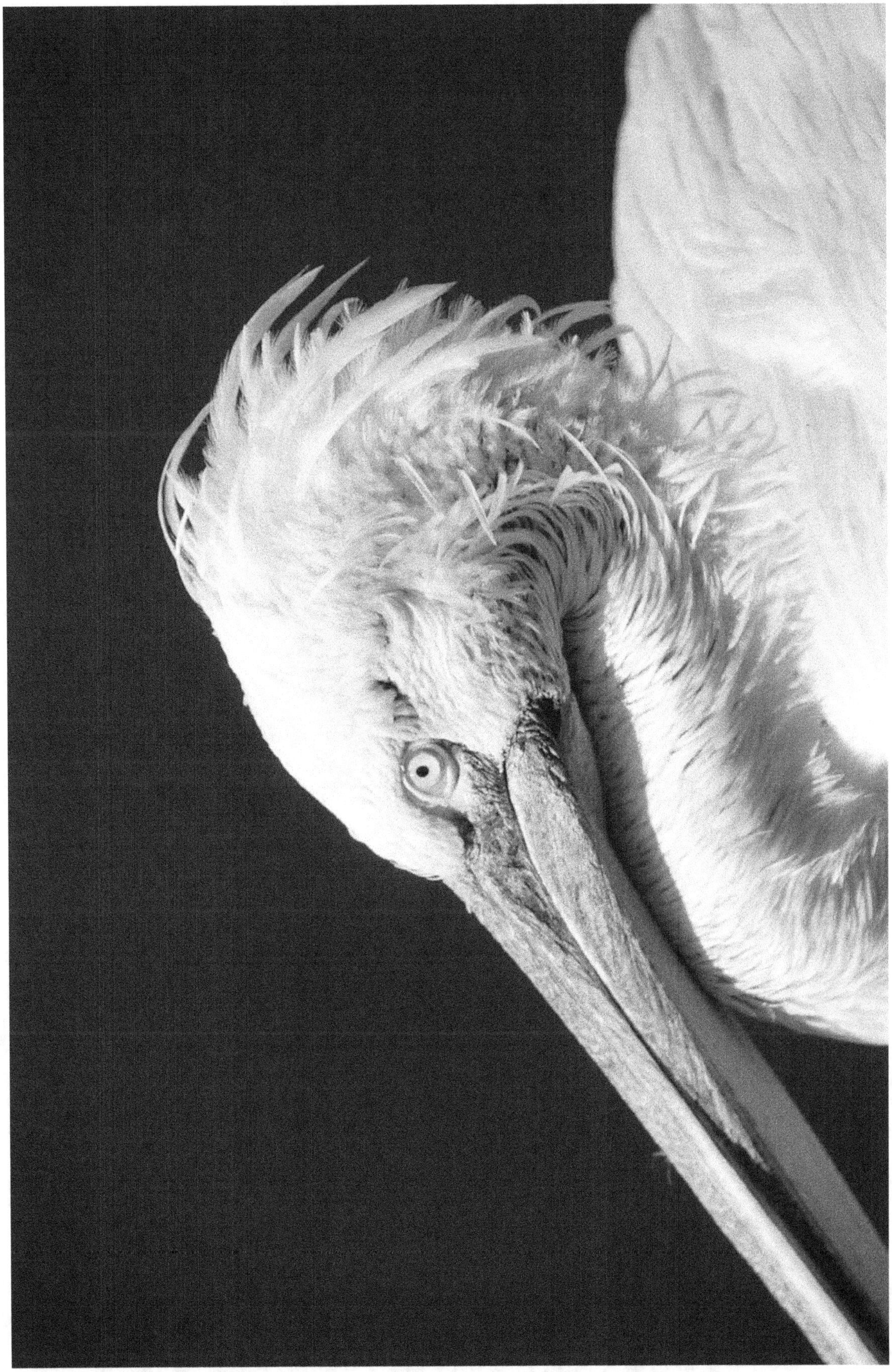

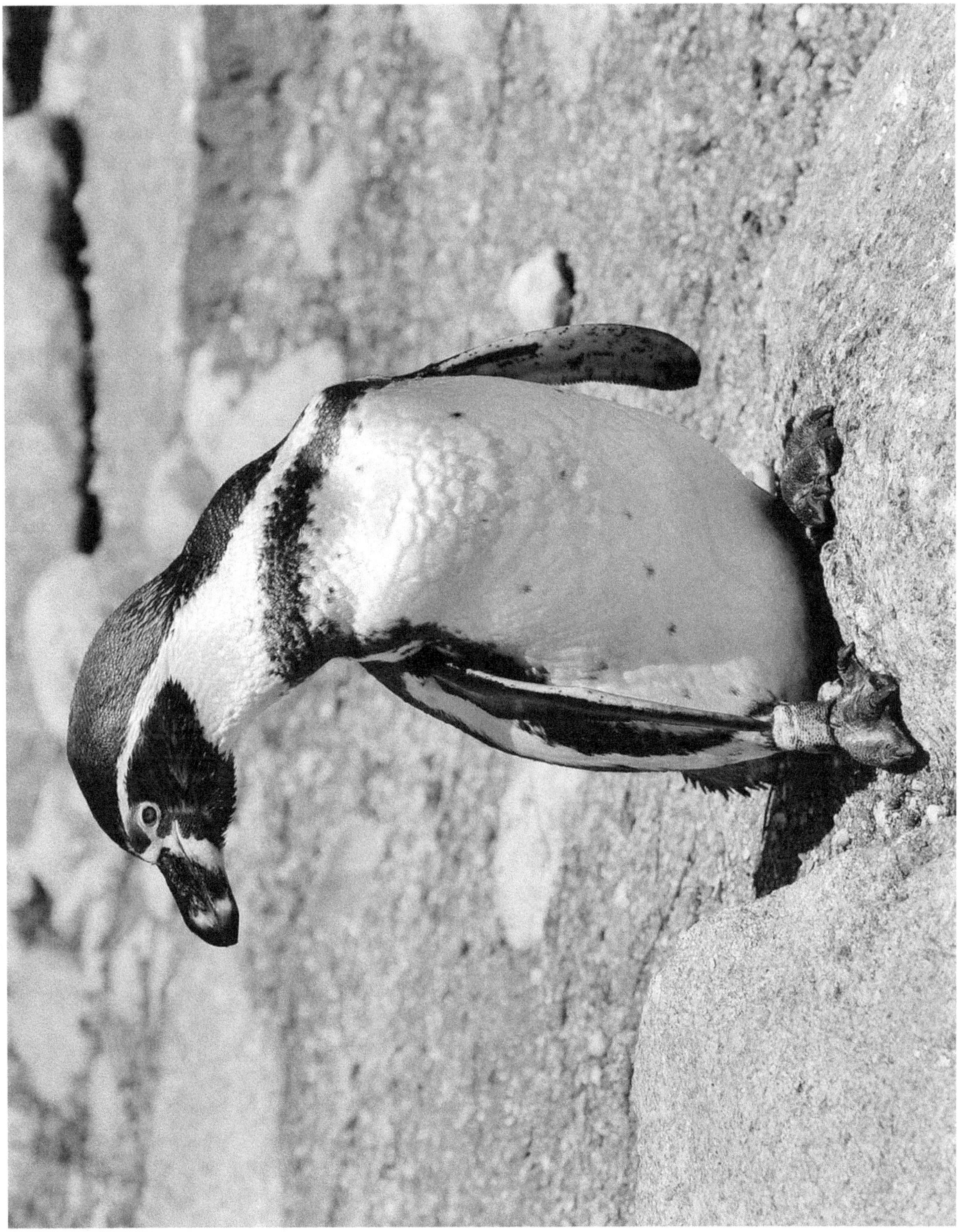

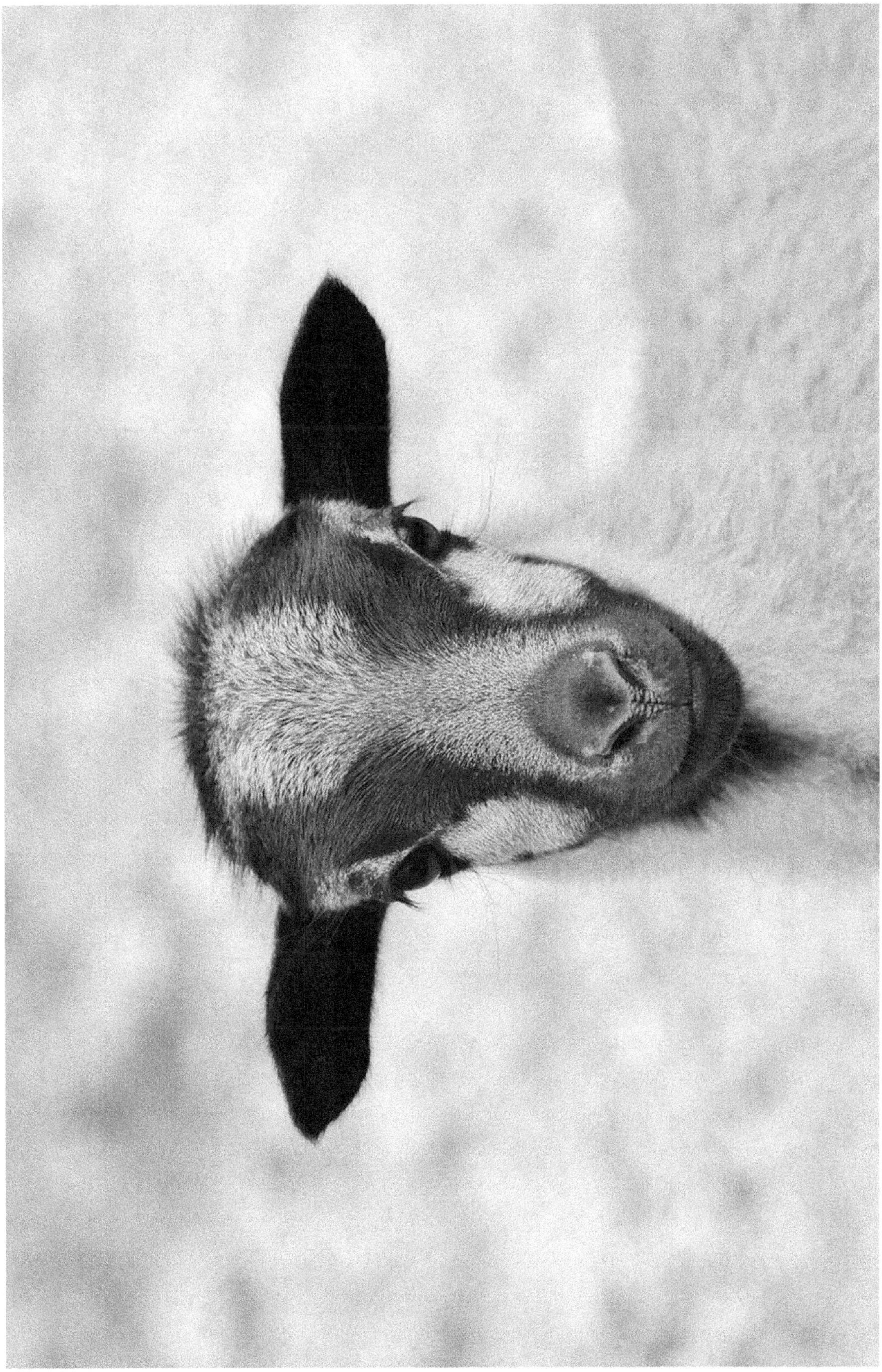

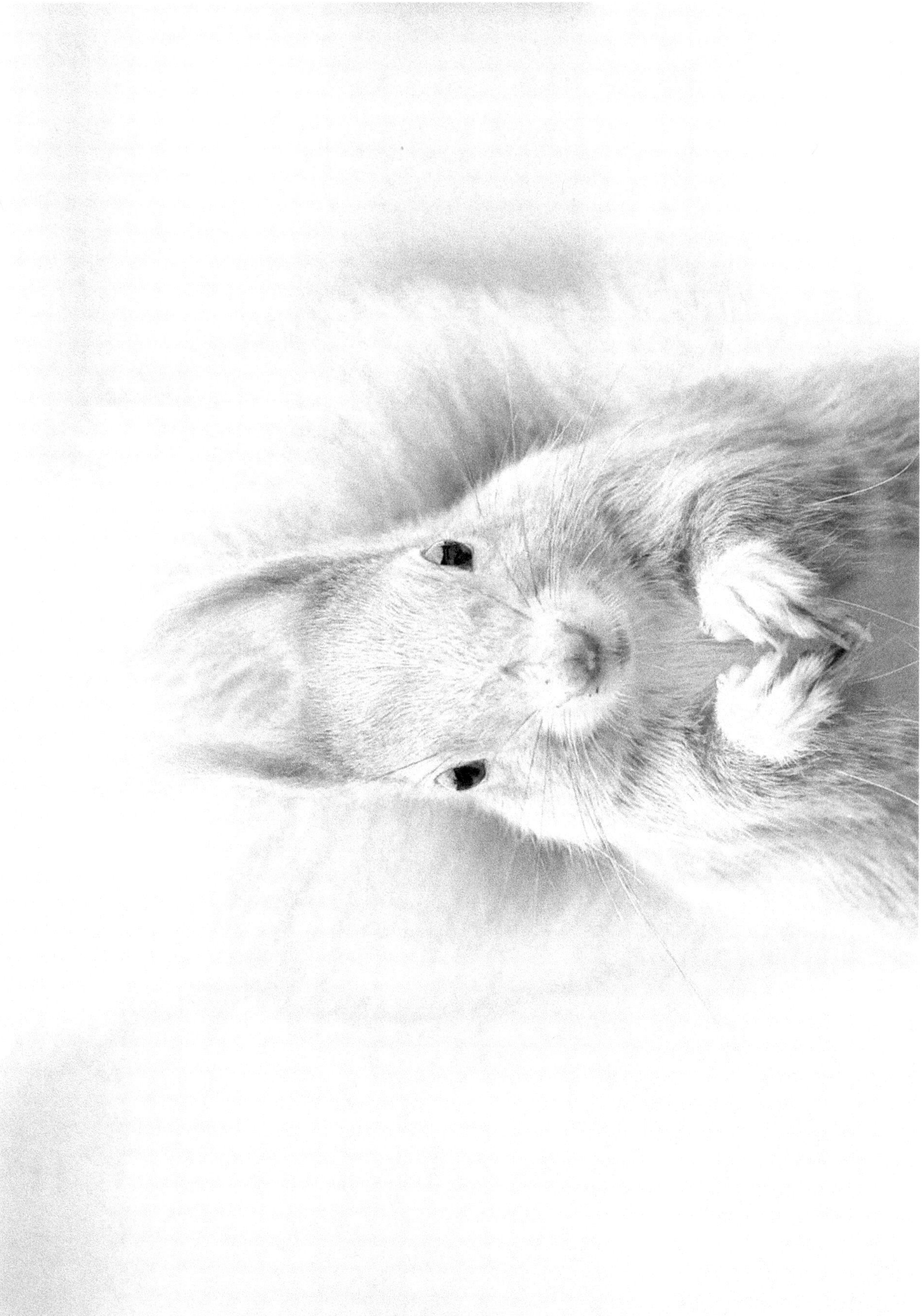

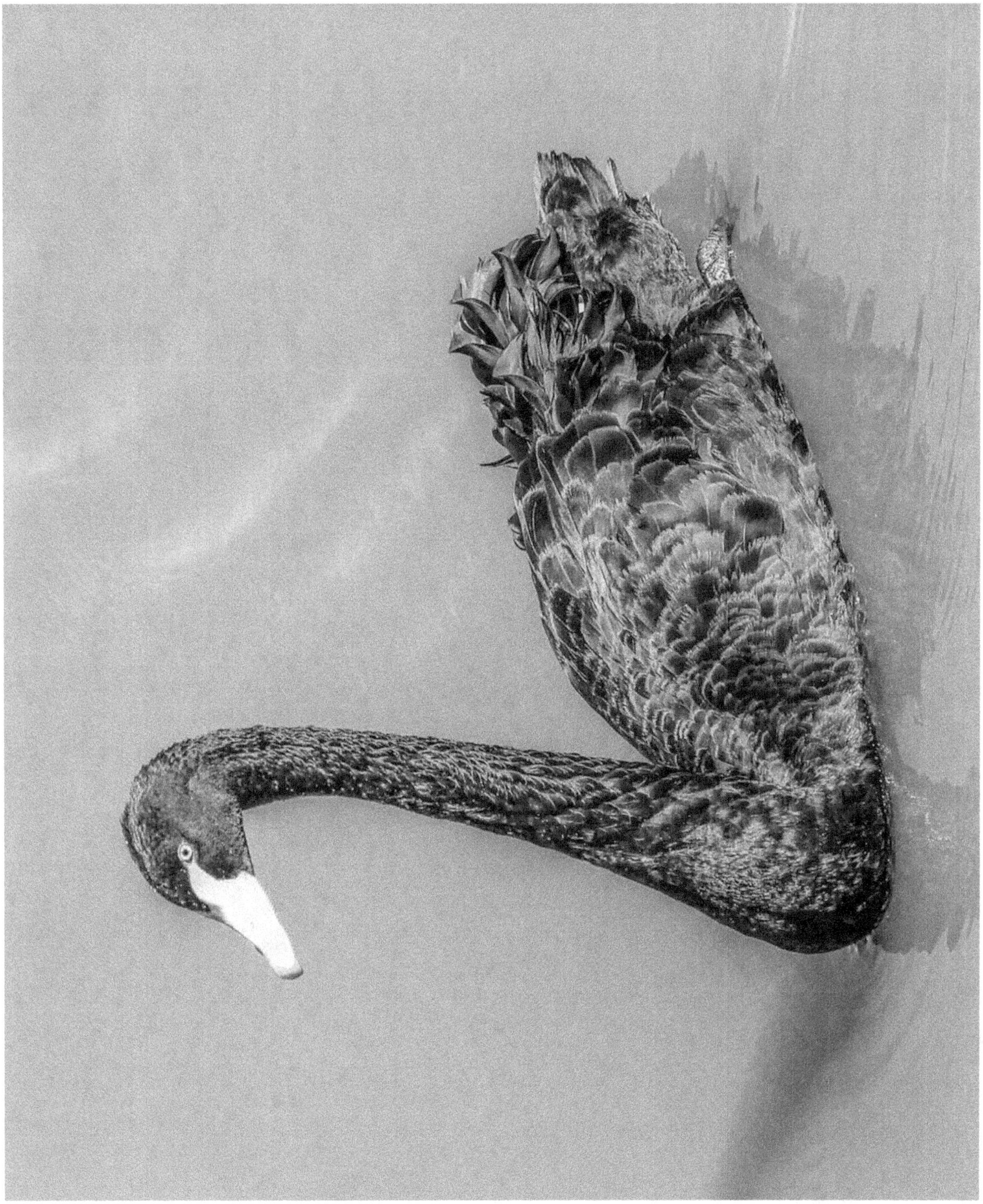

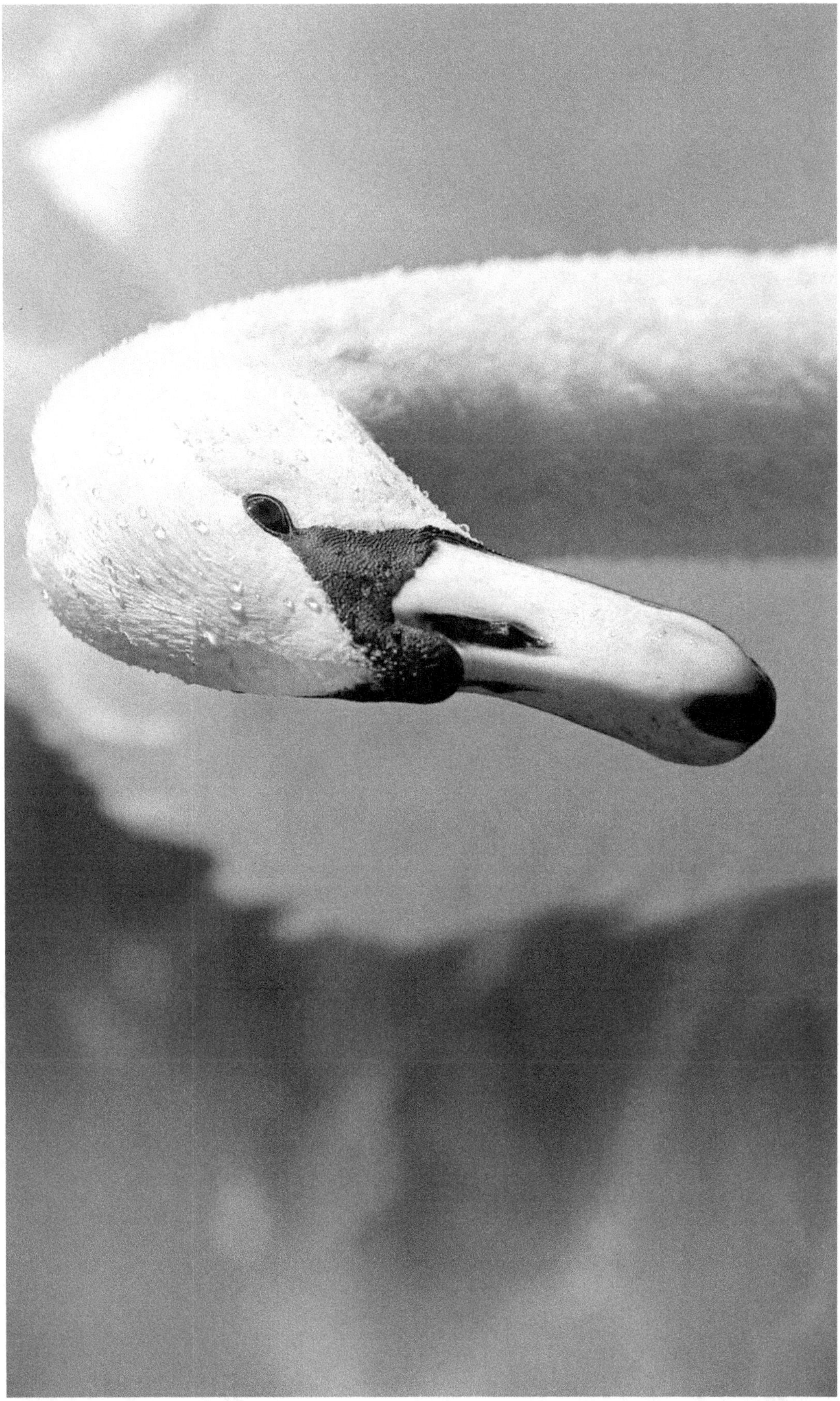

www.ingramcontent.com/pod-product-compliance
Lightning Source LLC
Chambersburg PA
CBHW081120280526
45787CB00007B/2915